What Do You Know About
The American Revolution ?

PowerKiDS press™

New York

Lynn George

Published in 2008 by The Rosen Publishing Group, Inc.
29 East 21st Street, New York, NY 10010

First Edition

Editor: Joanne Randolph
Book Design: Kate Laczynski
Photo Researcher: Nicole Pristash

Photo Credits: Cover, pp. 5, 6, 8, 9, 10, 11, 12, 13, 14, 15, 16, 17, 18, 19, 20, 21 © Getty Images; p. 7 © North Wind Picture Archives.

Library of Congress Cataloging-in-Publication Data

George, Lynn.
   What do you know about the American Revolution? / Lynn George. — 1st ed.
       p. cm. — (20 questions: history)
   Includes bibliographical references and index.
   ISBN 978-1-4042-4186-2 (library binding)
   1. United States—History—Revolution, 1775–1783—Miscellanea—Juvenile literature.
2. Children's questions and answers. I. Title.
   E209.G465 2008
   973.3—dc22
                                             2007031103

Manufactured in the United States of America

Contents

The American Revolution

What do you know about how the United States came into being? Did you know it took a war for the United States to become a free country? That war was called the American Revolution.

The United States started as a group of British **colonies**. Most of the time, Britain and the colonies got along. However, things changed in the mid-1700s. Britain tightened its control over the colonies. It forced **colonists** to pay more taxes. Colonists became angry. Soon war broke out between the colonies and Britain. When it ended, the colonies had become the United States of America.

During the war, the colonists realized that their new country needed a flag. Here Betsy Ross is showing the first flag to George Washington and his advisers.

1. Are the Native Americans on our side or France's side?

Britain and France claimed some of the same land in North America. That led to the French and Indian War, which lasted from 1754 to 1763. Indians, or Native Americans, fought for both sides. The British won. However, the war had cost a lot. Britain had many debts. Britain also had to keep **soldiers** in the colonies. To get more money, Britain raised the colonies' taxes.

This battle of the French and Indian War was fought in 1755.

Colonists were angry about the new taxes. They felt Britain had no right to tax them since they had no **representation** in the British **parliament**. They said there should be "no taxation without representation."

Here some colonists meet to protest, or speak out against, the British.

One tax law that angered colonists was the Stamp Act. Parliament passed this law in 1765. It said colonists had to pay for a tax stamp on things made of paper. Newspapers, papers having to do with the law, and even playing cards had to have tax stamps. Colonists **rioted**. Leaders from nine colonies met in New York City. They decided that taxes did not have to be paid unless the colonists agreed.

People from all the colonies were angry about the Stamp Act. Here an angry group protests in the streets of New York City.

Some **patriots** formed secret groups called the Sons of **Liberty**. These groups planned public gatherings and riots to show their anger over the Stamp Act.

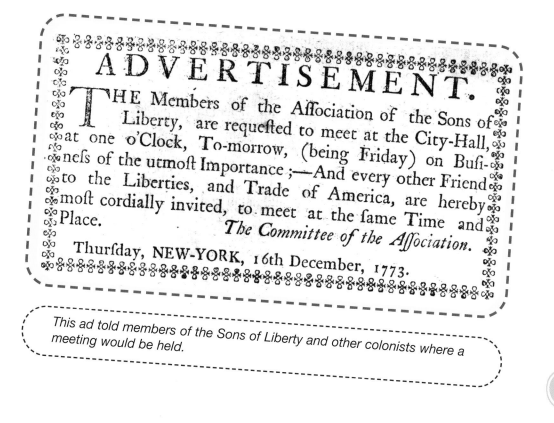

ADVERTISEMENT.

THE Members of the Affociation of the Sons of Liberty, are requefted to meet at the City-Hall, at one o'Clock, To-morrow, (being Friday) on Bufinefs of the utmoft Importance;—And every other Friend to the Liberties, and Trade of America, are hereby moft cordially invited, to meet at the fame Time and Place. *The Committee of the Affociation.*

Thurfday, NEW-YORK, 16th December, 1773.

This ad told members of the Sons of Liberty and other colonists where a meeting would be held.

In March 1770, a fight broke out between British soldiers and a crowd of colonists in Boston. Five colonists were killed and six were hurt. News of the Boston **Massacre** spread through the colonies. Colonists became even angrier with the British.

Paul Revere made this picture of the Boston Massacre. The picture was printed and given out to colonists to spread news of the event.

Like the British, colonists enjoyed drinking tea. Then Parliament taxed it. Angry colonists refused to drink tea. Shop owners refused to sell it. In 1773, a group of Boston patriots dressed up like Native Americans. They went onto British ships in Boston Harbor and threw all the tea into the water. This became known as the Boston Tea Party.

The Boston Tea Party took place on December 16, 1773. It sparked other acts of protest throughout the colonies.

Parliament decided it must stop the patriots. It sent soldiers to catch the patriot leaders in Massachusetts and destroy the patriots' arms. Paul Revere and William Dawes rode horses to tell patriots in Lexington and Concord that British soldiers were coming. Samuel Prescott joined them at Lexington. Only Prescott reached Concord to tell the patriots there.

On April 18, Paul Revere raced on horseback to let the colonists know that the British soldiers were on their way.

Paul Revere worked as a silversmith when he was not helping the Sons of Liberty.

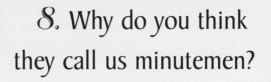
The members of the Lexington and Concord **militias** were not soldiers. They were just men who would fight to guard their town when needed. Special groups of militia members were picked to be ready at a minute's notice, so they were called minutemen.

Here minutemen get ready to march to Lexington and Concord.

9. Will war begin at Lexington and Concord?

British soldiers reached Lexington and Concord on April 19, 1775. Minutemen were waiting. After some fighting, the British turned back. Fighting continued as the British returned to Boston. When it ended, about 273 British and 95 minutemen were dead. The war had begun.

Minutemen faced the British soldiers on Lexington Green.

British soldiers fought with the minutemen on Concord Bridge.

10. Was the shot really heard around the world?

Ralph Waldo Emerson wrote that the first shot fired in the revolution was "heard 'round the world." This is not really true. However, the colonists were fighting for liberty and that idea spread around the world.

11. Who said women cannot fight?

Women were soldiers and **spies** in the war. Some famous ones were Deborah Sampson, Molly Pitcher, Lydia Darragh, and Nancy Hart.

12. Shall we let George do it?

Colonial leaders met in May 1775. They formed the Continental army. They made George Washington the army's leader.

Before the revolution started, George Washington fought in the French and Indian War. He also served in Virginia's government.

13. Then why do they call it the Battle of Bunker Hill?

After the British returned to Boston, the patriots decided to trap the British in the city. On June 17, the patriots planned to **attack** from Bunker Hill. Instead, they set up on Breed's Hill. The patriots lost the battle, but the British lost a lot of men.

The Declaration of Independence listed why America wanted to be free from Britain. It also listed the rights of the American people.

In 1776, the Colonial leaders asked Thomas Jefferson to write the Declaration of Independence. It said the colonies were a free country, called the United States of America. The declaration was signed on July 4, 1776.

Not all colonists were patriots. Many did not care who won the war. Many others backed the British. They were called loyalists because they remained loyal, or true, to Britain.

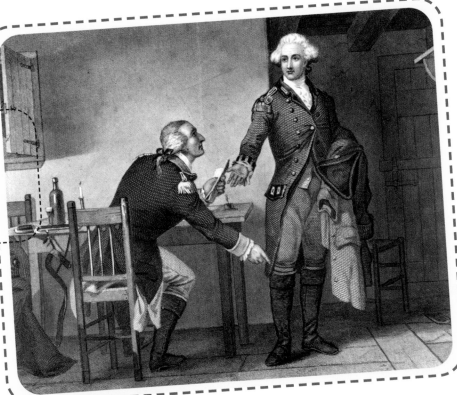

Benedict Arnold is best known for giving American secrets to the British. Before this, he had been an important leader in the American army.

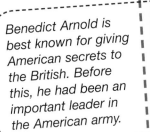

16. Why did Washington cross the Delaware?

The patriots seemed almost beaten by the end of 1776. British soldiers had chased Washington's army out of New York, into New Jersey, and then into Pennsylvania. The British thought they had pretty much won the war. However, Washington and his soldiers surprised the British. They crossed the Delaware River on Christmas night to reach an enemy camp. They caught about 900 sleeping soldiers.

George Washington's idea to cross the river at night was a daring one. It also helped give many colonists hope that they could still win the war.

17. Now do you believe we can win the war?

France secretly gave the patriots money and arms. However, it would not send soldiers. Then, the patriots won an important battle at Saratoga, New York, in October 1777. After that, France sent soldiers and ships.

The Battle of Saratoga was a turning point for the Americans. Here British general John Burgoyne surrenders, or gives up, to American general Horatio Gates.

The last big battle of the war took place near Yorktown, Virginia, in October 1781. American and French soldiers beat British soldiers. After this, the British knew they had lost the war. Britain was the world's most powerful country. It was shocked about losing. After the Battle of Yorktown, British soldiers played a song called "The World Turned Upside Down."

Here the British are shown trying to surrender to the French at Yorktown. The British still did not think of the American army as a real army.

Some fighting continued after the Battle of Yorktown. However, leaders from Britain and the United States met in Paris, France, in 1782. Both countries signed the **Treaty** of Paris in 1783. The war was over.

The young United States needed a government. Forming one was a hard job. In 1787, leaders from every colony except Rhode Island met in Philadelphia, Pennsylvania. They worked for months. At last they reached an agreement. They wrote a paper telling how the government would be set up. This paper is the U.S. Constitution. We still use the Constitution today.

Glossary

attack (uh-TAK) To start a fight with.

colonies (KAH-luh-neez) New places where people move that are still ruled by the leaders of the country from which they came.

colonists (KAH-luh-nists) People who live in a colony.

liberty (LIH-ber-tee) The state of being free.

massacre (MA-sih-ker) The act of killing a large number of people or animals.

militias (muh-LIH-shuz) Groups of people who are trained and ready to fight when needed.

parliament (PAR-lih-mint) The lawmakers of a country.

patriots (PAY-tree-uts) American colonists who believed in separating from British rule.

representation (reh-prih-zen-TAY-shun) People who have been picked to speak in government for all the people.

rioted (RY-ut-ed) Acted in a way that is disorderly and out of control.

soldiers (SOHL-jurz) People who fight in a war.

spies (SPYZ) People who watch the enemy secretly.

treaty (TREE-tee) An agreement, signed and agreed upon by each party.

Index

B
Britain, 4, 6–7, 18, 21–22

C
colonies, 4, 6, 8, 10, 17, 22
country, 4, 17, 21

F
France, 6, 20, 22

M
militia(s), 13

N
Native Americans, 6, 11
North America, 6

P
parliament, 7–8, 11–12

patriots, 9, 11–12, 16, 18–20

S
soldiers, 6, 10, 12–15, 19–21
Stamp Act, 8–9

T
tax(es), 4, 6–8
Treaty of Paris, 22

Web Sites

Due to the changing nature of Internet links, PowerKids Press has developed an online list of Web sites related to the subject of this book. This site is updated regularly. Please use this link to access the list:
www.powerkidslinks.com/20his/amrev/